Welcome to Motherhood

By Lori Fettner

Published by Sunrise Media, LLC

A wise mom knows when to ask for help. I am grateful to my husband, Mike, for supporting my writing, and being my partner in life.

A special thanks to my good friend Andrea, and to everyone else who contributed photos of their beautiful families.

Much appreciation to my parents, Joyce and Sy, and in-laws, Reena and Lee, who gave me the tremendous gift of time, without which I couldn't have finished this book (or done laundry!)

And of course, for Hannah, the inspiration for it all.

For:

From:

Message:

My personal reflections on motherhood:

Welcome to Motherhood

For months you haven't had a good night's sleep.
When will baby sleep through the night?
But when she finally does get a solid 8 hours,
All you can think is, "this can't be right."
This is the moment you've been waiting for,
A chance to finally get some rest.
But you spend all night in a panic,
Staring at her chest.
Is she okay? Is she breathing?
Why won't she just make a sound?
Welcome to motherhood,
Where the contradictions abound.

Another moment you've been waiting for…baby's first steps!
At last, at last!
Are these tears of joy or sorrow?
They grow up so fast.
Just yesterday she was too afraid to let go,
Reaching for my hand.
Suddenly she just got up and grinned,
So proud that she could stand.
My baby is standing, I thought as I filmed.
But this moment didn't last long.
That's when she took off walking,
And I'm trying to be strong.

How can I feel all these emotions at once?
Being a mom is so strange.
You want them to grow up,
But you also don't want a thing to change.
You desperately need a break,
But miss them the second you leave.
You want them to be independent,
But miss the tugging on your sleeve.

How will you feel when they begin to drive?
When they go to college or move away?
I can't think about that right now.
I'm not letting go of today.

The Secret to Not Washing Dishes

The baby finally fell asleep, now I can curl up with a glass of wine.
The sink is full of dishes, but I'll deal with them some other time.
Before settling in, I put my dinner plate on top of the pile.
I manage to clean off the table once in a while.
Turns out, that last plate was one too many for the stack,
And as I let go, I hear a loud CRACK.
My favorite wine glass has broken in two at the bottom of the sink.
Now I really need a drink.
I get so attached to my things, the old me would have been heartbroken.
I would have spent the next few weeks looking for the exact same token.
But now I can't help but smile as I think, "Oh my gosh,
That's one less glass to wash!"

Motherhood Defined

Baby's crying forcing you out of bed.
Always having a fun song stuck in your head.
Cleaning up lots of poo.
Melting at every smile and coo.
Eating cold dinners that used to be hot.
Really appreciating everything you've got.
Watching her tear your favorite book in half.
Playing games and loving her little laugh.
Looking for the remote and car keys she took.
A little girl climbing into your lap with a book.
Being exhausted pretty much all of the time.
Being amazed that this kid is actually mine.
Feeling like you've lost yourself and are now "just" a mother.
Knowing a pure love that is really like no other.
The bad is nothing compared to the good.
And there's really no way to define motherhood.

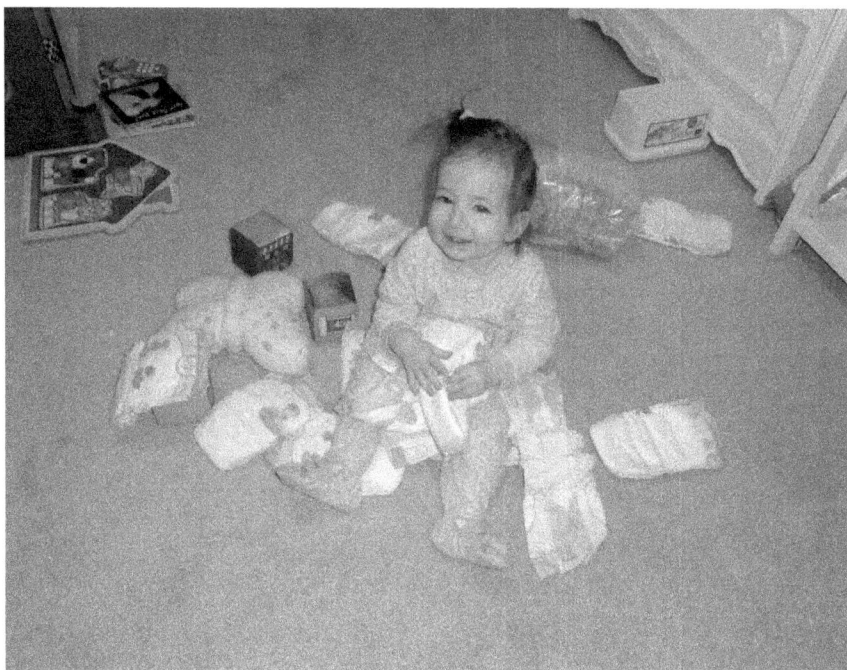

A Spicy Mistake

You know whatever you eat, he does too,
But I forgot and ordered chicken vindaloo.
I couldn't believe my eyes or ears,
My normally delightful baby was in tears.
Maybe he's hungry, I thought, so I nursed.
That only seemed to make it worse!
I felt awful as he looked at me with his tear-soaked eyes.
And he now had terrible gas to go along with his cries.
This was when I realized the fault belonged to me,
Spicy Indian food and my baby did not agree.

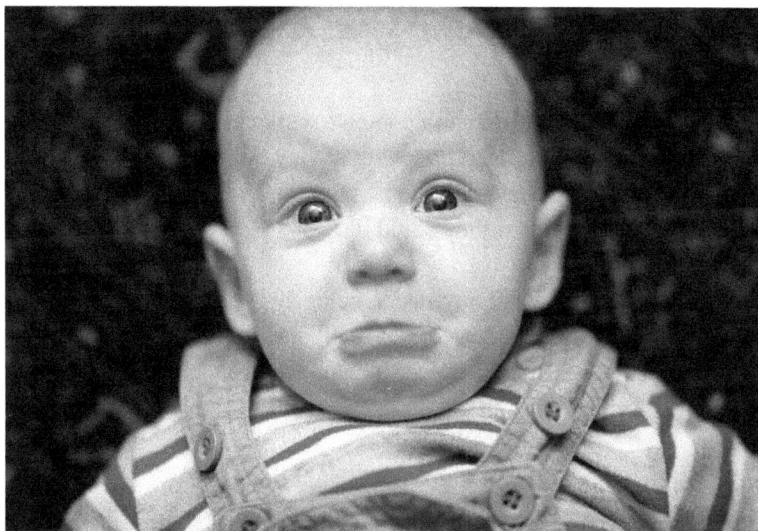

Mom Guilt

As a stay-at-home mom I just can't compete with what she'd get at daycare.
Professionals and other kids to play with all day, it just doesn't seem fair.
Am I being selfish in keeping her home with me?
Are her days really the best they could be?

Working moms don't have it any easier, being away from their kids all day.
They make money but wonder, does it really pay?
They are sometimes torn in their decision and wonder if they're missing out.
Mom guilt is torture, without a doubt.

We constantly wonder if we're doing the right things.
Did we stay in too much, should we have gone on the swings?
Or was it wrong to take her out in the cold?
This is how kids get sick, I've been told.

Did I dress her too warm, or not warm enough?
How am I supposed to know all this stuff?
We're new at this, and babies don't come with directions.
Let's just try to remember, they'll likely survive our imperfections.

Date Night

Hubby and I are getting a night out.
But first I have a day to get through.
How will I get ready while caring for baby?
This is something I'm not sure I can do.

I'll take advantage of every break I get.
The baby needs to nap well so I can shower.
Nap time comes, and into the shower I run.
And I'm lucky to get a whole hour!

Now comes the tricky part.
It's two and I'm not off the clock until five.
It will take skill to stay date-ready for three whole hours.
I stay in my sweats, knowing my dress wouldn't survive.

The first hour flies by,
And I brace myself for snacktime at three.
The milk goes down smoothly,
But most of her carrots end up on me.

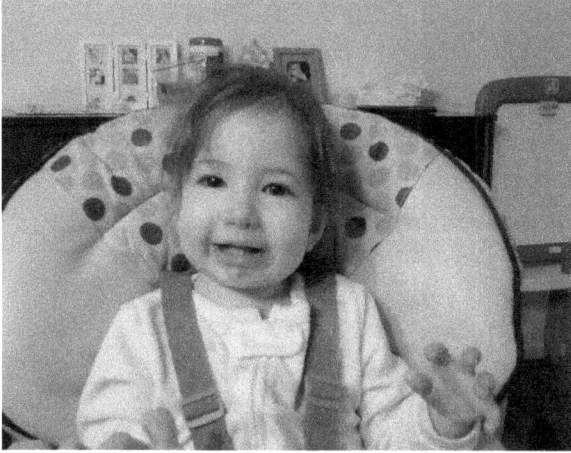

By the time five rolls around and my sitter arrives,
I'm about ready for a nap.
I get dressed and take a peek in the mirror.
And realize I look like crap.

Carrots still on my face, something green on my neck.
And my shoes don't match. Didn't I check?
The baby has been pulling and tugging on my hair.
I'm afraid the curls are beyond repair.

I find shoes that match, and pull my hair back with a sigh.
I wash my face, and looking at the time, decide to let it air dry.
I'm sweating now and out of breath, my shower feels like decades ago.
But hey, a night out is still a night out, and I'm all ready to go.

Weight

Why did I just have Chinese buffet?
I've been so concerned with how much I weigh.
I promised myself no more crème brulee,
But I have no self control at the end of the day.

I'm busy all day, but it's not exactly exercise.
Washing dishes is doing nothing to help my thighs.
Nursing has helped reduce my size
But with it comes a hunger I can't deny.

When baby is older, I'll do more active things,
Take him for walks, push him on the swings.
I'll lift him up and down as if his legs were springs
And run with him in my arms, his arms spread like wings.

All this will happen in good time.
So if I can't get to the gym now, is it really such a crime?
Right now there are bigger things on my mind.
So, if you've noticed I haven't yet lost my baby weight, please be kind.

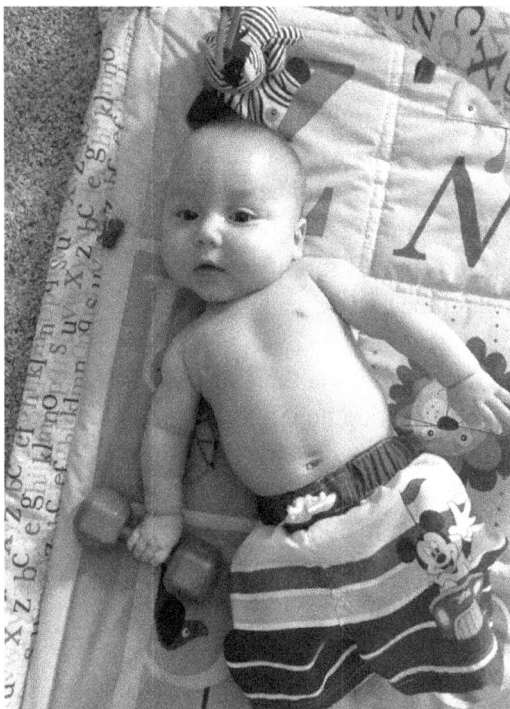

Sick

A Tribute to Shel Silverstein

"I cannot go to story time today,"
If my daughter could talk is what she'd say.
She's coughing, won't sleep, and has a runny nose.
Her ears are itchy and there's hair on her toes.
She's squinting, and I'm not sure if she can see.
What on Earth can it be?
I'm not one of these moms who over-reacts,
But there's some crazy stuff out there, that's a fact.
With parents not vaccinating their kids these days,
It could be measles, mumps, or some brand-new plague.
I look in her mouth and her tonsils seem blue.
I really don't know what to do.
I finally decide to give the doctor a call.
When he asks for the symptoms, I list them all.
He says, "It's the first time your child is sick, if I can be so bold."
"I really think it's just a cold."

Precious Naptime

I'm not normally selfish but I need to be,
Naptime is when I shower, eat, and pee.
Time and again I am doing these selfish things,
When of course the telephone rings.
"Baby's asleep, so I thought it would be a good time to call."
"You're wrong," I think to myself, "Damn it all!"
Why does this phone call upset me so?
When baby gets up, she'll be ready to go.
If I don't eat and rest (and maybe also shower and pee)
There is no way I'll keep up with her energy.
You might think all we do is sit around and play.
But this is my only break in a 12 hour day.
So, while it would be nice to talk to you without a baby tugging at the phone,
I simply do not want to waste these precious few moments I have alone.
So please do call me when the baby's awake,
I'd rather not talk during my break.

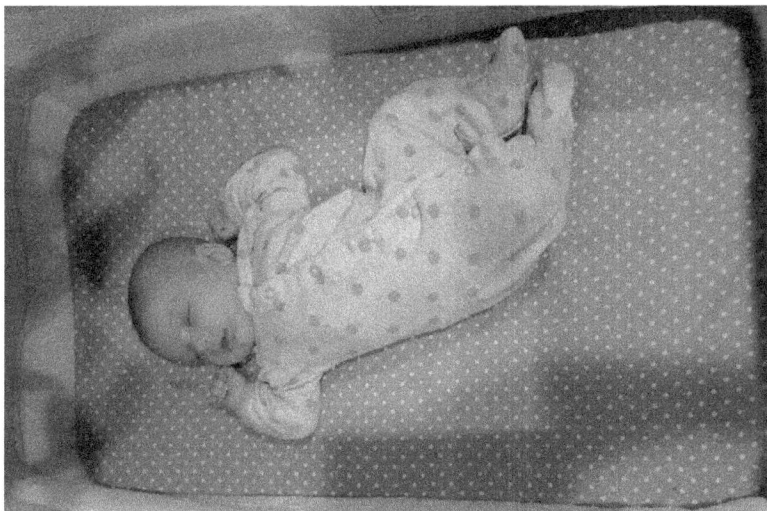

Shhhh

The smallest of sounds never seemed so loud.
I actually cringed when my cat meowed.
I tiptoe past the baby's room and the floorboards roar.
I think the whole house shook when I closed the door.
The woodpecker's peck is like a sledgehammer.
That squirrel eating a nut is creating quite a clamor.
The wind outside sounds like thunder.
When did the world get so loud, I wonder.
There were never this many planes overhead.
Every time I hear one I'm filled with dread.
And while I'm too afraid to vacuum or even sweep,
My baby is immune to it all, soundly asleep.

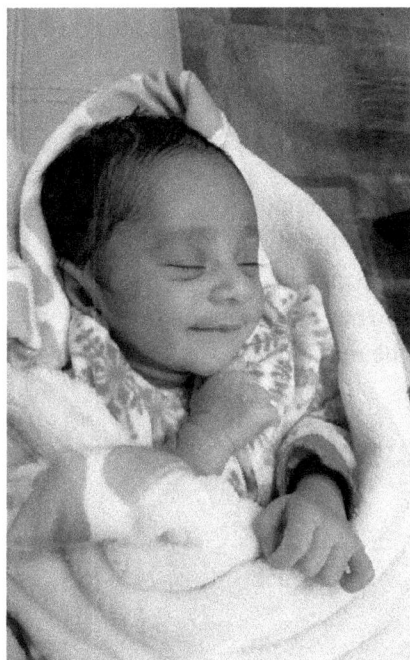

Sleepover

Baby and grandma are having a sleepover.
What should I do to prepare?
Let's start with a list of reminders:
Don't let baby sleep with a clip in her hair.
Next I'll put together her schedule
So grandma knows when she sleeps and eats.
I type up this and the reminders,
And it comes to about a dozen sheets.

Now let's get her suitcase
And begin to pack.
What clothes will she need?
I'll just throw in the whole rack.

I pack up her toys
And all of her food.
I pack extra for grandma,
I wouldn't want to be rude.

I finish up with the big items:
Her couch, chair, and crib.
And think of more small things
Like her books, spoons, and bib.

I carry everything downstairs,
Tired now and glad I don't have to drive too far.
But there's one thing I forgot to consider:
How will I fit this all in the car?

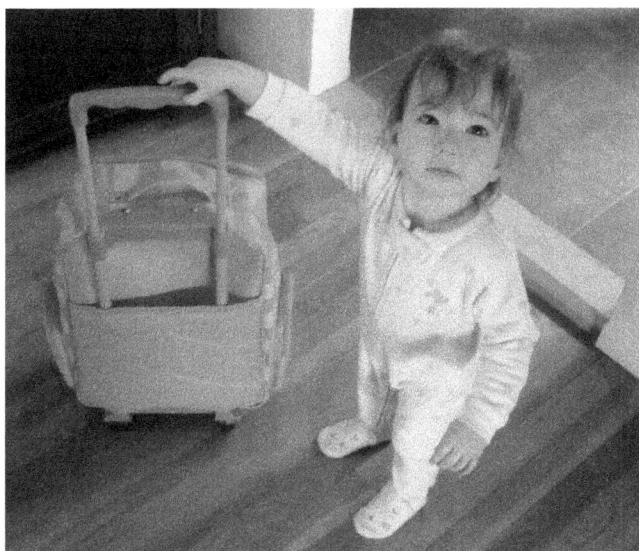

Toys Toys Toys

Ever been woken by an elephant singing in the middle of the night?
Toys that wake themselves up just aren't right.
It's great that they turn on when the baby crawls by,
But in the dead of night, it just makes me want to cry.
New parents, be sure to turn off all toys before you go to sleep.
Or you may be woken by a toy car screaming "beepity beep."

And now on to some battery advice:
Have plenty of extras, or you will pay the price.
When the swing is the only thing that puts your baby to sleep,
Seeing it slow to a stop will surely make you weep.
You'll feel even worse if you can't find your Double A's.
At that point, you'll just want to pray.

In addition to batteries, always have a screwdriver nearby.
If you're a new parent, you're probably wondering why.
It's because you're now in a childproof world
And without a screwdriver your battery-changing plans will be unfurled.
You never know if you'll need a phillips head or a flat.
I bet you never thought you'd have to think about that.

Did you ever think there would be so much to learn about toys?
And we haven't even gotten to noise.
Before buying any toy make sure it has a volume control
With some toys, keeping your sanity is the goal.
If these new toys really drive you up the wall,
He might have the most fun with a good old fashioned quiet ball.

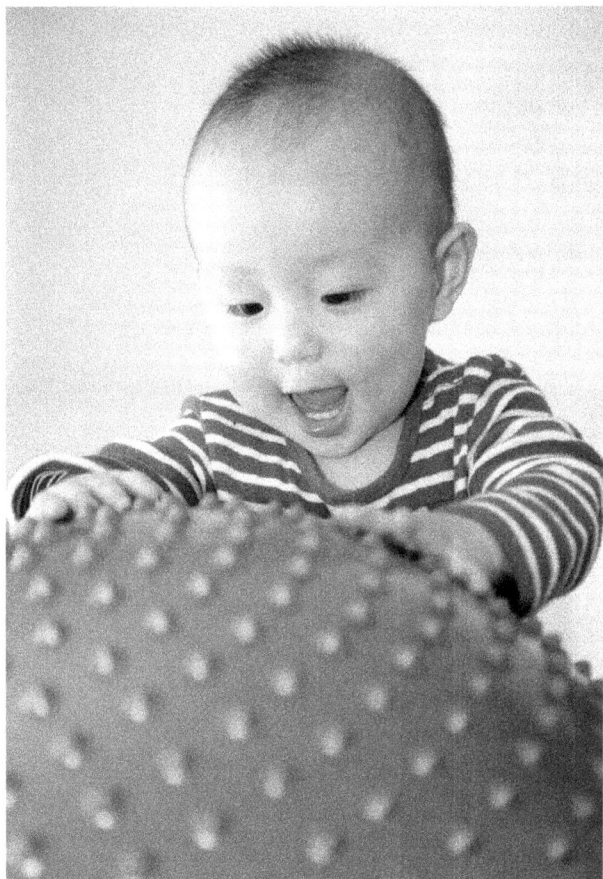

It's Okay

Did you put the laundry in but forget to take it out?
It's okay.
Do you sometimes feel overwhelmed and full of doubt?
It's okay.
Is the house not as clean as you'd like it to be?
It's okay.
Is this job harder than you thought it would be?
It's okay.
Do you sometimes miss the life you had before?
It's okay.
Do you sometimes think of the baby as yet another chore?
It's okay.

Trust that there will be amazing days as well as the bad.
Days with overwhelming joy, and those when you're sad.
Having a baby is life-changing, so feel what you need to feel.
You can hide away your thoughts, but it's better to be real.

So, whatever you're feeling it's okay.
Just keep taking it day by day.

Nursing Dilemmas

Baby always cried around eight and I couldn't figure out why.
The doctor said every baby is cranky at night and it's normal for them to cry.
I trusted him, but this just didn't seem right.
I finally learned that I produce less milk at night.
My baby wasn't getting enough to eat, how was I to know?
I started pumping in the morning to help out when my supply was low.
This solved the problem, but why is there so much to nursing that no one tells you?
Do people feel it's some rite of passage a woman must go through?

The next problem arose when I introduced a bottle so I could go out for a bit.
It was still my milk, but baby would have none of it.
It wasn't what she was used to, and she cried and cried.
She wouldn't drink from a bottle no matter what I tried.
Until she took that bottle, I had to stop nursing and pump all her meals.
This worked, but it was quite an ordeal.
One bottle a day early on is the way to avoid this.
I wish all the nursing coaches hadn't been so remiss.

The final problem I had is a common one.
For some women nursing is over before it's begun.
The rules for producing enough milk are pretty detailed,
But some women don't know this and feel like they've failed.
Avoid alcohol and drink tons of water and mother's milk tea.
These rules enabled me to nurse exclusively.
It also helps to pump in the morning and save it for when your supply is low.
That also helps your body keep producing as your baby's hunger begins to grow.

I hope by giving you this information,
It will help you avoid some frustration.
If nursing isn't for you, that's okay,
But if it's what you really want, don't let anything stand in your way.

Tired

Have you ever been so tired, you just didn't know what to do?
Having a baby tends to do this to you.
With so little sleep, you can't tell up from down.
You forgot to water the plants, and now they're all brown.
After awhile you think you are fine, but couldn't be more wrong.
You put so many things where they just don't belong.

Just today, I hung my coat in the shower,
Powdered my feet with flour.
Brushed my hair with a wrench.
And what is that stench?
Oh no, I just poured salad dressing in my tea,
What on Earth is wrong with me?

I'll tell you what's wrong, I'm just tired you see.
Really paying attention is the key.
Thinking you're okay is the biggest mistake.
Realize you can't function well when you're not awake.

You put your food in the oven, but did you turn it on?
Go double check while you yawn.
And when the meal is cooked, make sure you turn off that flame.
Don't be embarrassed, lack of sleep is to blame.
It's better to be safe than sorry, as they say.
Don't worry, you'll get to sleep again one day.

Unexpected Thoughts

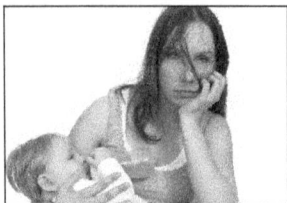

After a day with the baby, I look forward to getting out for a bit.
I'll even take out the garbage while hubby gets a chance to sit.
He'll be so happy to play with baby for awhile
And I'll mow the lawn with a smile.
I'll get the mail and wash the dishes, and I'll consider it a break.
Daddy can have a turn playing patty cake.
The two can also play a game of hide and seek,
While I go under the sink to finally fix that leak.
These are normally chores that no one wants to do,
But there's only so much one can take of peek-a-boo.

After a long day at work, the last thing I want is to do chores,
But it's all got to get done before I walk through that door.
I haven't seen my little girl all day,
But all this work stands in my way.
I take out the trash, get the mail, and mow the lawn.
Then I collapse on the front steps with a yawn.
The baby is going to bed soon, how is this fair?
A working dad doesn't have a minute to spare.
I wish there were more hours in the day.
I wish there was time for me and the baby to play.

Dad walks in to an angry mom who wants to know where he's been.
Dad doesn't even know where to begin.
He's angry now too and the couple realizes they need to work this out.
They decide to talk instead of scream and shout.
Dad never thought mom would want to do those tasks.
And mom never realized all she had to do was ask.
Dad would gladly spend some time with his daughter.
While Mom took some time to get things in order.
The couple never realized things could be so great.
It's a good thing they decided to communicate.

Spitting Image

"She has her daddy's eyes," says Aunt Jane.
"And my beautiful smile," beams Uncle Dan.
"She has my teeth, all six of them," says Cousin Joe.
"And she has my dimples," boasts Aunt Anne.

When she eats well, she takes after Aunt Beth.
When she spits it all out, she's just like Grandpa.
Energy after a meal belongs to Aunt Joyce.
And when sleepy, she's just like her Grandma.

"She's playful like me," says the dog.
"And curious like me," says the cat.
"She has my laugh," says Grandpa Sy.
And Cousin Mike says, "I used to blink like that."

Even folks who aren't related think my baby has their traits.
I guess we're all lacking a little modesty.
Because I simply nod and smile,
Knowing my baby is just like me.

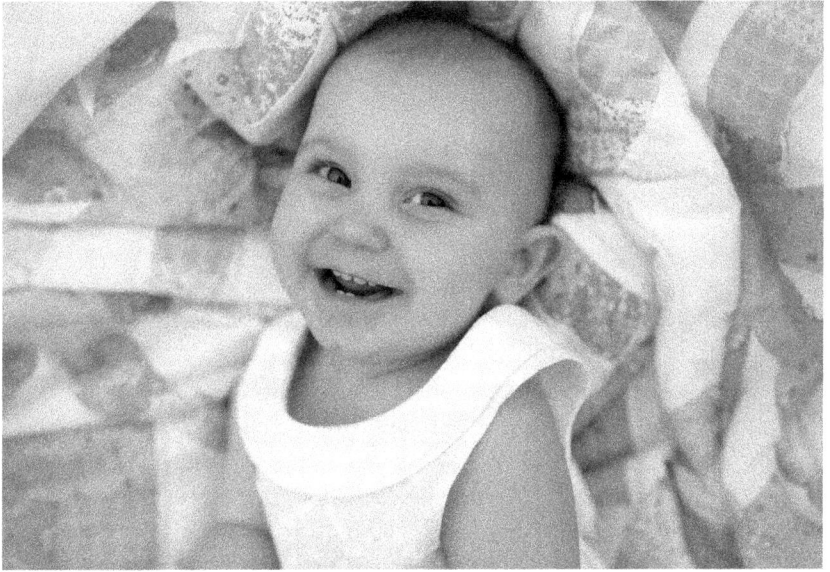

Scheduled Baby

Some would call me crazy
I set an alarm to wake up my baby.
Wake up a sleeping baby, you say.
Yes, this is how I start my day.

My baby is on a schedule and I never hear her cry.
There's a plan for her meals and naps on which she can rely.
Keeping to a schedule is a bit of a sacrifice,
But if you saw how great my baby is, you wouldn't think twice.

I can't help but brag when asked how well my baby sleeps.
She goes from 8 to 8, hardly making a peep.
The response I get to this is pretty much a dare:
Brag about the first child, and the second will be a nightmare.

I sometimes wonder if it's the schedule or if my baby is just really good.
I'm thinking of doing an experiment . . . maybe I should.
Raise the second child without a schedule, do I dare?
Nope, I don't want my second child to be a nightmare.

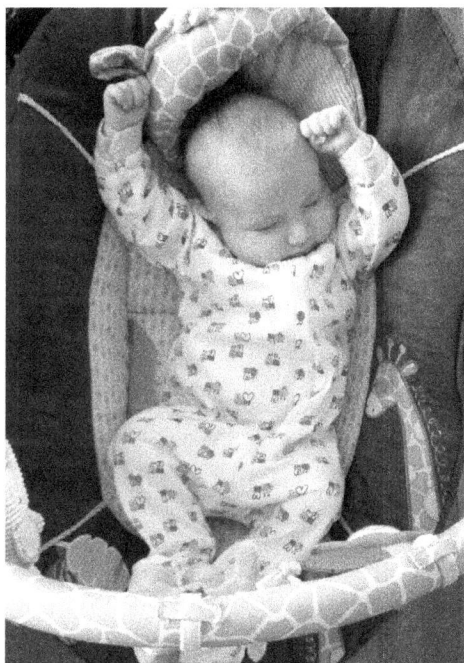

Ready for Another?

People are so happy when you have a baby
They feel they can ask you anything that's on their mind.
Are you nursing? Does she sleep?
Do you and your husband ever get to unwind?

The one question that surprises me the most
Is one I wasn't ready for at all.
When are you having another, they ask.
"Um . . . ," I think of ways to stall.

I just had a baby,
And you already want me to have another?
I don't even know what I'm doing yet.
I just became a mother!

It would be nice to finish having babies all at once.
That's one advantage to having kids close in age.
Potty trained, starting school, and out of the house,
A quicker end to every stage.

It would also be nice for my little girl to become a big helper.
That's one good reason to wait.
Help sorting laundry, washing dishes, and caring for the baby,
Wouldn't that be great?

I could weigh both sides,
But the fact is right now I simply can't think of having another.
The world will just have to wait
For my little girl to get a sister or brother.

Worth the Wait

When baby is first born, it can be quite distressing.
You feel overwhelmed, while everyone else says "It's a blessing."
The life changes you've made can be really tough.
But there will be some rewards soon enough.

The first of these is baby's first smile.
That'll begin to make your efforts feel worthwhile.
Next she may laugh, babble, and coo.
This should make you feel a little less blue.

If you're still feeling down
Just wait until she's crawling around.
You may now feel like your work's just begun,
But chasing her around can be pretty fun.

It was shortly after this that things really changed for me.
It wasn't a baby, but a little girl that I began to see.
She now climbs into my lap, cozy and snug.
And runs over to me to give me a hug.

Words can't describe how amazing this feels.
I went from feeling pretty blah to being head over heels.
I can't believe how much different I feel from just a year ago.
It really is a blessing, but how could I know?

Parting Words

The days are long, but the years are short
I once heard someone say.
It didn't make sense to me then
But I totally get it today.
I get up in the morning
And think of all the hours I have to fill.
I have to educate and entertain all day.
And of course we can't stay still.
We go for walks and to the parks and playgrounds
When it's nice outside, there's plenty to do.
But on rainy days, the minutes tick by.
And that's how the first half of the saying is true.
As for the other half,
Well, as the end of this book is near,
I can't believe how fast my daughter has grown.
It's been an entire year.
How could the year have gone so quickly
When I've been watching the minutes tick by?
All I can say is, hold on to each moment, both the precious and painful
Because time really does fly.

About the Author

Lori Fettner was a production editor in the children's division of Simon & Schuster before becoming a teacher, and now she is writing full time while caring for her daughter. Her first book, Teaching to the Child, was published under the penname Ms. Frank in 2012.

Lori is currently working on the 2nd book in her motherhood series.

Visit LoriFettner.com for more information on her past and upcoming books, events in your area, her teaching and motherhood blogs, and more!

Book 2 in the Welcome to Motherhood series: The Toddler Years

Tips and humor about potty training,
a reassuring voice when your baby has their first bad dream,
and much more!
Visit LoriFettner.com for more details,
and enjoy this sneak peak now

Bad Dream

My daughter woke up crying
And had no words to tell me what was wrong.
She could only lift her arms up and whimper
While I tried to calm her with a song.

My daughter woke up crying
So I carried her to our favorite chair.
She snuggled in the crook of my arm
And fell asleep while I held her there.

My daughter woke up crying
This hasn't happened in so long.
She's almost 3 now and can talk,
But couldn't tell me what was wrong.

My daughter woke up crying
I think she had her first nightmare.
How can I protect her from what's in her own mind?
And will I ever know what gave her this scare?

My daughter woke up crying
Part of her innocence is gone
I'm not sure what to say or do.
For now, I'll just hold her until dawn.

Car Seat Struggles

For the past several months, I've had so much trouble getting my daughter into her car seat. She arches her back, kicks her legs, and screams. This doesn't happen every time, but always at the worst times…when I am late for an appointment, or just plain tired and wanting to go home. Today I found something that worked. It may not work tomorrow, but it worked today. I'll first list all the failed ideas, then reveal today's success. Feel free to skip to the end.

1. "We're going to see_____, we just need to get in the car." (fill in the blank with something exciting, but be honest!)

2. Talking her through it with praise: "I'm going to put you in the car now. You're going to be a big girl and help me buckle you in. Then we're going for a drive."

3. Letting her play outside for a few minutes before trying to get her in.

4. Trying to put her in directly from the house (with no play time first.)

5. Letting her walk up to the car herself.

6. Carrying her to the car.

7. Threats. "If you don't get in the car nicely, I won't be able to take you _____ anymore."

8. Outsmarting your toddler/team work with your partner. With two people, one can help from the back seat while the other stands outside by the car seat. When by myself, getting her in through the side, sitting in the back seat, sometimes worked better than trying from the outside.

9. Bribery. "I'll give you _____ if you get in the car." These last two work, but not quite the best parenting.

And here is what I came up with today:

I put a small stuffed animal in the car, not her favorite, just one she likes. The "bear" now lives in the car, and we only get to see him if we get into the car seat nicely. On several trips out today, my daughter walked over to the car saying "bear, bear," and I had no problem getting her into the seat. She got to hold the bear while I strapped her in, and then willingly handed the bear back to me when I was ready to go. I then tucked the bear out of sight and we were on our way. I was surprised I didn't get screams of "mine" when I asked for the bear back, maybe that's something I have to look forward to another day. But for today, we had success, and I've learned to take these things one day at a time. I don't know why I didn't think of this sooner. Seems so obvious now. I'll try to think of using this type of reward system in the future.

Maybe you've had the same car seat struggles, or maybe you're struggling with something else. I hope this post gives you hope that you'll soon find a strategy that works...for at least one day anyway.